Table of Contents

I0559658

Scripture quotations are from the ESV® Bible (The Holy Bible, English Standard Version®), © 2001 by Crossway, a publishing ministry of Good News Publishers. Used by permission. All rights reserved. The ESV text may not be quoted in any publication made available to the public by a Creative Commons license. The ESV may not be translated in whole or in part into any other language.

ISBN 978-1-998048-09-0

Walk This Week With Jesus

Jesus called His disciples with a simple invitation, "Follow Me." For us, His invitation stands. Today, we do not have the privilege of pacing with Jesus over dusty paths, but we follow Him still. We are to follow His teaching, His example, His Voice and His purpose. This devotional invites you to journey with Jesus through the Passion Week, the days from Palm Sunday to Easter morning.

This was a week that changed time and eternity. Heaven and history celebrate what God did in those 7 days. Over one third of the Gospel chapters are devoted to the events of that week. Since the Gospel writers thought those days were so important, we ought to give them similar attention. You are encouraged to hover over the Bible texts found in this devotional. You will see some people worshiping Jesus and others challenging Him. You will hear Jesus teach of things to come and things that are. You will eavesdrop on the intimate conversation of our Lord around the Last Supper. You will witness His suffering and the fearful confusion of His followers. You will marvel once more at the empty tomb.

It's likely that you will not read anything new. This booklet is not intended as an instructional seminar, but a devotional. Engage the Bible texts with your heart. Imagine standing there, what would you think and feel? What questions or fears would you have? What hope arises from these texts? What do you want to say to Jesus? Allow the Spirit of God to refresh and rekindle your soul.

You may wish to utilize this devotional through the Passion Week, one day at a time, leading you to Easter morning. Each day will offer the Gospel accounts, collected to give a sense of what took place. Read those Gospel verses as if for the first time. Additionally, there is a brief mediation on the Bible narrative of that day. Take time to reflect on God's truth and engage in prayer, giving God your intentions, trust, frailty, gratitude and love. You will also find a portion of the Psalms. Consider memorizing the verse to hold onto God's promise throughout the week.

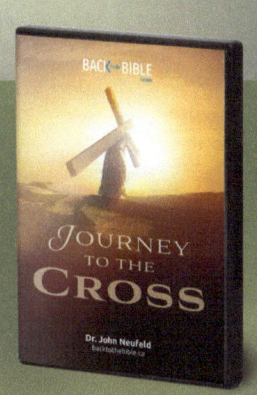

For those looking for more teaching on this week, we invite you to listen to Dr. John Neufeld's preaching series, *Journey to the Cross*. You can access it through the website of Back to the Bible Canada at **backtothebible.ca**

A Week That Was Planned

 Today's Bible Reading: John 11:1-12:11

 Setting the Stage:

A Few Days Before...

Most of us have two days in a 24-hour span. There is the day we planned and the day we get. Those two do not necessarily coincide. We can be surprised and frustrated by distractions and the unexpected. We learn quickly that there is much outside of our control. We end up responding to situations rather than commanding them. Not so with Jesus.

The events of the Passion Week were not a surprise to Jesus. This was not a week that spun out of control. Every circumstance of these days was saturated with the intent and purpose of God. The sovereign Lord orchestrated the "Who? What? When? and Where?" He has the wisdom, power, and authority to direct this week towards His, "Why?" That is evident with the death of Lazarus.

When Jesus heard that Lazarus His friend had died, He delayed (John 11:6). Why? The Passover was near, and Jerusalem would be filled with worshippers. Jesus raised Lazarus from the dead at a time of heightened publicity. He prayed at the tomb so that all would know that the Father sent

Those who saw this miracle filled Jerusalem with the news. Many came to faith that He was the Messiah.

Him (John 11:42). Those who saw this miracle filled Jerusalem with the news (John 11:45-57). Many came to faith that He was the Messiah (John 11:45). His enemies became focused on killing Him (John 11:53). The curious began to look for Him during the Passover (John 11:56). None of this was accidental. Jesus was conducting His actions at this time and in this manner, for optimum impact. In less than a week, Jesus would enter Jerusalem riding upon a colt, declaring Himself to be the expected Messiah. Those that had witnessed the raising of Lazarus led the city in praise, "Hosanna!" (John 12:17-19). The city was primed and prepared for the events of Passion Week. God was in control and Jesus walked in obedience.

What of us? How are we to respond to God's governing Hand upon our world and in our days? Consider the example of Mary (John 12:1-8). John writes of Mary's devotion evidenced with great sacrifice and deep humility. She anoints Jesus with pure nard and wipes His feet with her hair. It was the fragrance of her gratitude for raising her brother back to life. It was the scent of worship that would linger upon Jesus, even until His crucifixion and burial. Mary did not understand why Jesus delayed coming to help her sick brother. Mary would have felt confused and overwhelmed through the events about to unfold. But this she could do; she would worship Jesus, trusting Him throughout. We can do the same.

Mary would have felt confused and overwhelmed... But... she would worship Jesus, trusting Him throughout. We can do the same.

 Time to Reflect and Journal:

- What stands out for you in these verses?
- What is God's invitation for your life?
- What do you want to answer back to God in prayer?

Palm Sunday
Entrance of the King

 ## Today's Bible Reading:

Matthew 21:1-11, Mark 11:1-11, Luke 19:28-44, John 12:12-19

> ### Key Memory Verse: Psalm 24:7-8
>
> "Lift up your heads, O gates! And be lifted up, O ancient doors, that the King of glory may come in. Who is this King of glory? The Lord, strong and mighty, the Lord, mighty in battle!"

 ## Setting the Stage:

Jesus Leaves No Doubt

A reader of the Gospels may wonder, "Why didn't Jesus make it obvious who He truly is?" At times, Jesus seemed to be coy. He taught with parables that confused the crowds. He cautioned some He healed to tell no one about it. He withdrew from a crowd intent on making Him king. He ministered in backwoods Galilee, removed from the major centre of Jerusalem. It's not that His words or identity were hidden, but neither were they proclaimed - until now.

Palm Sunday is Jesus' purposeful proclamation. When Jerusalem was buzzing about the raising of Lazarus, Jesus chose to fulfill Zechariah's prophecy that Israel's Messianic King would come riding on a colt (Zechariah 9:9). He delegated two disciples to obtain the colt and began a descent on the Mount of Olives into the city. It was the spark to release the energy of anticipation within Jerusalem. Palm branches were broken and laid on His path for a parade of praise. The crowd sang Psalm 118:26, *"Blessed is he who comes in the name of the Lord!"* People erupted with "Hosanna!" Their King had come! Jesus did nothing to stop them, as if they were mistaken. Instead, when some Pharisees objected and wanted the disciples to stop, Jesus replied that stones would replace their silence. Even creation would proclaim, *"Jesus Christ is King!"*

What matters here is Jesus' declaration, not the crowd's sincerity. This was the revealing hour in which Jesus left no doubt as to who He was. He was making a statement with no ambiguity. Jerusalem needed to know that the Messiah was in their midst. Did everyone believe? Time would sift the faithful from the mere enthusiastic. In a few days the same voices would call out, "Crucify Him!" Jesus was not fooled by the crowd's adulation. He knew what was to come.

Jesus Weeps

Tears reveal our hearts. A person's hopes, wounds and love can be so large, they spill out their eyes. Luke records a very intimate snapshot of Jesus. Nearing the city with the noise and excitement growing, Jesus wept. He knew most of their worship was fleeting. He cried for the suffering in store for the people of Jerusalem. The city that welcomed Him would be destroyed. People's celebration would turn into lamentation. Jesus cried for the judgement to come upon them. He shed tears over an opportunity for deliverance spurned. He grieved over what could have been.

Jesus shed the tears of a parent watching their child stride towards disaster. Advice offered is ignored. Help is rejected. Affirmations of love fall on deaf ears. The beloved will reap problems and pain when it wasn't necessary. Does it hurt the parent? Supremely. Is their love diminished? Their tears say otherwise. Jesus cries for the city which rejects Him. The Lord longed to envelope them with mercy and grace, as a mother hen shelters her brood under her wings (Luke 13:34). But the people would not have it. Jesus cries for a city which spurned Him. Jesus cries today for our resistant hearts which ignore His Word and ways. His love is in His tears.

 Time to Reflect and Journal:

- What stands out for you in these verses?
- What is God's invitation for your life?
- What do you want to answer back to God in prayer?

Today's Bible Reading:

Matthew 21:12-13, Mark 11:12-19, Luke 19:45-46

> ### Key Memory Verse: Psalm 139:23-24
>
> "Search me, O God, and know my heart! Try me and know my thoughts! And see if there be any grievous way in me, and lead me in the way everlasting!"

 Setting the Stage:

Not as It Should Be

At the end of Palm Sunday, Jesus entered the temple and looked around, but since it was already late, He left for Bethany. Something Jesus saw in the temple weighed on Him all night long. It was revealed in His words and actions on Monday by cursing a fig tree and cleansing the Temple. He was teaching us something.

On the way, Jesus approached a fig tree, lush with leaves but barren of fruit. It was not the season for figs, but regardless, Jesus condemned the tree and declared its barrenness to be permanent. On Tuesday morning, the disciples would pass the tree once more and see that it had withered to its roots.

When Jesus came to Jerusalem and entered the Temple, He created havoc! Passover required that worshippers sacrifice a lamb. It was convenient for those who traveled far to purchase an animal in the Temple. This required Temple currency, so tables were set up to make the money exchange. Jesus had seen all this the night before and now He would put a stop to it. He threw the tables upside down and chased the merchants from the Temple. He barred any more dealers from entering. His actions not only shocked the worshippers, but it cemented the intentions of His enemies to kill Him (Mark 11:18). Critics have suggested that Jesus was simply in a bad mood that day. Cursing trees and venting at those doing their jobs. What is this all about?

Jesus is speaking and acting as a prophet to Israel. He is challenging the worship of the nation. Like a fig tree, which looks fine from a distance, the life of the Temple worship was fruitless. It had the look of godliness but did not produce the expectations of God. Temple worship was arranged for the convenience and profit of people and merchants, but the essentials were missing. Jesus quotes Isaiah 56:7 that the Temple ought to be a place where nations gather for prayer and worship. It was to be a welcoming beacon for all to worship God in prayer. But the Temple courtyard of the Gentiles was crowded with a system to accommodate the Jews.

The nations were squeezed out.

And of Us?

It's hard to miss our own corporate reflection in Jesus' words. We attend church Sunday by Sunday and become accustomed to the manner of our services. Most congregations are a mixture of things to applaud and things to avoid. Yet these two prophetic words from Jesus must be considered. If our worship looks good from a distance but proves to lack the fruits of God's Spirit, things need to change. If our churches are shaped more for the comfort and ease of believers than an invitation and welcome of the nations for God's glory, things need to change. Our worship should not be barren, nor should it be more about us than God's heart for all people.

On Monday, Jesus points to what God intends worship to be. He was about to give His life to make it so. May it be so among us.

 Time to Reflect and Journal:

- What stands out for you in these verses?
- What is God's invitation for your life?
- What do you want to answer back to God in prayer?

Tuesday
A Challenging Day

 Today's Bible Reading:

Matthew 21:20-23:39, Mark 11:27-12:44, Luke 20:1-21:38

Key Memory Verse: Psalm 119:130

"The unfolding of your words gives light, it imparts understanding to the simple."

 Setting the Stage:

"Got Ya!" Questions

Jesus returned to Bethany Tuesday morning. He entered Jerusalem and went to the Temple, where merchant tables were back in place. You can imagine the concern of Temple officials and the curiosity of the crowds, "What would Jesus do today?" While no tables were thrown, it was a day filled with challenges, debates, and questions.

His opponents were intent on trapping Jesus. They couldn't deny His miraculous power and saw that His actions and words were attracting public applause. They reverted to an old tactic that is as current as today's journalism. They threw "Got Ya" questions at Jesus. A "Got Ya" question is intended to trap someone into making a statement that would discredit them publicly. The questioner is not interested in soliciting a full truthful answer. Tuesday was filled with questions thrown at Jesus to make Him look bad.

They wanted Jesus to justify disrupting the Temple. "By whose authority do You do these things?" They wanted Him to get into trouble with the Roman government. "Should oppressed Jews pay taxes to their oppressors?" The Sadducees who denied the resurrection hoped to snag Him with a theological question. "If a woman dies with 7 previously deceased husbands, whose wife will she be?" The Pharisees step up next and, as experts on the Law, ask Jesus, "What is the greatest commandment?" Every question was a trap. Every question had a large audience of listeners. Every question was answered by Jesus with wisdom and truth.

As to His authority, Jesus reversed the question and asked them about John the Baptist's authority. He knew they wouldn't answer for fear of losing favour before the crowds. As to paying taxes, Jesus said the answer is on the coin itself. "Give to God what is God's and to Caesar what is Caesar's." The convoluted scenario of marriage in the resurrection was resolved with Jesus' clarity. "There is no marriage after the resurrection and God is the God of the living." Even the Pharisees could not deny the accuracy of Jesus' answer about the greatest commandment. "You shall love the Lord your God with all your heart and with all your soul and with all your mind." Finally, as the day ended, "No one was able to answer him a word, nor from that day did anyone dare to ask him any more questions" (Matthew 22:46). His opponents had been verbally pinned to the mat.

Minds Shut Tight

In all of this, the clarity and wisdom of Jesus should have moved many towards faith. He answered their every question and challenged them with teaching of His own. His enemies had to admit that they were bested in the debate, yet they did not change their minds about Him. They were corrected but held to their mistakes. They were not seeking truth, so their erroneous convictions remained. The inability to see where we are wrong is called confirmation bias and it is real, even among believers. We may hold to our positions and rationalize our reasons despite the clear Word of God. Our hearts and minds can be stubborn. May they be pliable to the truth.

 Time to Reflect and Journal:

- What stands out for you in these verses?
- What is God's invitation for your life?
- What do you want to answer back to God in prayer?

Wednesday
A Retreat of Silence

 Today's Bible Reading:

Matthew 26:14-16, Mark 14:1-2 & 10-11, Luke 22:1-6

Key Memory Verse: Psalm 116:7

"Return, O my soul, to your rest;
for the Lord has dealt bountifully with you."

 Setting the Stage:

Jesus Goes Quiet

Wednesday of the Passion Week has been controversial. There has been much written and spoken about the events of Wednesday simply because it appears to be absent. There is no chronology within the Gospels which specifies Wednesday. The events jump from a Tuesday filled with challenges and Jesus' teaching to Thursday's preparation for the Passover. While Matthew 26 and Mark 14 seem to place Mary's anointing of Jesus on this Wednesday, it seems more likely that John's account of the anointing happening before Palm Sunday is accurate (John 12:1). He is the only one to specify a time for it, while Matthew and Mark may have written thematically. As there is no Gospel narrative for the Wednesday of Passion Week, what did Jesus do?

We know that Jesus was lodging at Bethany at the home of Martha, Mary, and Lazarus. It is likely that after the intensity of the past days, Jesus retreated with His disciples and friends. He needed to rest after the emotional drain of teaching daily in the Temple and facing the conflict with His enemies. He needed to rest for what He knew was coming. Wednesday was a day of both recovery and preparation. If the past pattern of Jesus directed His actions on this Wednesday, then we can assume that He spent some time alone in prayer. He may have had private conversations with each of His disciples who had followed Him for three years. Certainly, there was a communal meal filled with joy and love. It's instructive that Jesus goes quiet in the middle of the most important week of history. Jesus took time for self-care. There was more that could be said or done in the last week of His life. But Jesus didn't have to do everything, only what the Father wished. He was called to be obedient, not to maximize productivity.

The Devil Doesn't Rest

Not everyone rested. It is around this time that Judas makes contractual arrangements to betray Jesus. Satan had his grip on Judas and Judas yielded to his hand. Judas approached the chief priests and offered to be their means to arrest Jesus. Judas would seek the most opportune moment and deliver the Lord into their grasp. He would get 30 pieces of silver for his pocket. If this was a movie, the drama would be unmistakeable. Jesus is resting with followers and friends. Judas is conniving, conducting the Devil's deal, and trying to satisfy the greedy darkness of his own heart with money.

Evil doesn't rest. It is driven by demands for pleasure, power, and possessions. It is insatiable. Goodness can rest. Righteousness is marked by contentment. Godliness trusts the Hand of the Father. There is a Sabbath for the people of God. This Wednesday of the Passion Week reminds us that wickedness is constantly busy earning its final judgement. The ways of Christ invite peace and restoration, finding an eternal rest.

The ways of Christ invite peace and restoration.

 Time to Reflect and Journal:

- What stands out for you in these verses?
- What is God's invitation for your life?
- What do you want to answer back to God in prayer?

Today's Bible Reading:

Matthew 26:17-75, Mark 14:12-72, Luke 22:7-65, John 13:1-18:27

Key Memory Verse: Psalm 40:17

"As for me, I am poor and needy, but the Lord takes thought for me. You are my help and my deliverer; do not delay, O my God!"

 ## *Setting the Stage:*

Flooded Hearts and Minds

There are occasions that overwhelm us. They can be events of joy or pain that we pass through and struggle to absorb all that is happening. Thursday of the Passion Week was such a time for the disciples. Within the span of a day and night they prepared and celebrated the Passover with Jesus, were crushed and confused by the news of a betrayer in their midst, tried to embrace Jesus' promise of a new covenant, had Jesus wash their feet, heard His encouragement to not be troubled by His death, boasted of their brave loyalty, failed to pray with Him in Gethsemane, and panicked when soldiers with torches approached. Things got worse from there. Jesus was dragged away. Most of them ran to save themselves. Peter followed from a distance and witnessed the false accusations and physical abuse of his Lord. His fidelity crumbled into denial. Jesus was left alone to face the dawning wrath of religious hypocrisy and political self-interests. They would kill Him.

Final Words

John's Gospel has the most detailed account of what Jesus said to the Twelve through these events. Chapters 13-17 are a well so deep, it is hard to fathom. Yet we return to this section repeatedly for refreshment. Focus on chapter 14.

Despite the burden upon His own soul, Jesus cared for the turmoil of His disciples. It was His default to minister to those who would face trauma. The One about to die comforted those who would witness His death. To paraphrase His words, "Do not be troubled, have faith in God and in Me." It is the same encouragement Jesus extended to Martha and Mary at Lazarus' grave. It's the hope Jesus offered to Jairus at the news of his daughter's passing. Faith is the appropriate response to death. It is faith that enables the living to continue and to live on with comfort and hope.

Faith is not a pep talk, as if sheer emotion could elevate and empower us. There is content to faith, truth that is relied upon. What truths did Jesus offer these frightened men?

Again, a paraphrase:

"Even as you have trusted Me in these last years, trust Me now. The Father has not failed you or Me. He won't fail now. It is true that I am leaving, but I will come back to get you, so you can live with Me forever. In the meantime, I will send you a Helper who comes from the Father. He will live with you always, even to the depths of your soul. I won't leave you alone like an orphan. The Helper will bind you to Me and Me to you. You will know my love and that of the Father and the Helper. We will make Ourselves known to you. I give you peace, My peace, not a shallow comfort for the moment, but an unshakable confidence that fears or worry cannot withstand. So, welcome My leaving. I am going back to the Father, but I will never be far from you. This is not an ending, but the beginning of something far greater. Take hope in that."

 Time to Reflect and Journal:

- What stands out for you in these verses?
- What is God's invitation for your life?
- What do you want to answer back to God in prayer?

Today's Bible Reading:

Matthew 27:1-56, Mark 15:1-41, Luke 22:66-23:49, John 18:28-19:37

Key Memory Verse: Psalm 22:14-15

"I am poured out like water, and all my bones are out of joint; my heart is like wax; it is melted within my breast; my strength is dried up like a potsherd, and my tongue sticks to my jaws; you lay me in the dust of death."

 Setting the Stage:

A Terrible Price for a Terrible Crime

It has been preached, portrayed, expounded, explained, the theme for books, films, canvas, drama and poetry. For 2000 years the faithful and faithless have used their imaginations to grasp the events of Good Friday. It has yet to be exhausted. This much is clear. The tragedy of the event points to the seriousness of its cause.

We must not take a detached perspective as if the events of Good Friday didn't involve us. Despite the span of time and space, each one of us is the direct cause of Jesus' death.

"But he was pierced for our transgressions; he was crushed for our iniquities; upon him was the chastisement that brought us peace, and with his wounds we are healed. All we like sheep have gone astray; we have turned - every one - to his own way; and the Lord has laid on him the iniquity of us all."
(Isaiah 53:5-6)

The death of Jesus Christ was the atoning grace of God to cover and forgive all our sins. Our sins were placed upon Him and in return we received His righteousness by faith (2 Corinthians 5:21). The crimes belong to us. The punishment belonged to Him. In Jesus' death, we are shocked by the abuse He endured, the pains He suffered, the humiliation heaped upon Him. The extremity of the punishment ought to revolt us; for it points to the revulsion of our crimes.

No Small Things

We have a diluted vision of sin. It is common among us; done by us, done to us, done around us. Our familiarity with our fallen state immunes us to the weight of sin. We reserve our shock for the major offences found in media headlines. Yet our white lies, casual unkindness, verbal attacks, self-centered decisions, private lusts, prayerless days and withheld love all pass under the radar of our conscience. These seem like small matters, overlooked and inconsequential. But there is no inconsequential sin.

The holiness of God is absolute. It is the brilliance of purity without spot or shade. Our sins are a violation of who God is, what He demands and who He created us to be. Our sins are offences regardless of their size, impact, or intent. They not only harm us and others, but they also require a just response from God. The penalty for sin is death. The mercy of God has inserted His own Son into our place of condemnation. He died for us. The ugliness of His crucifixion reflects the ugliness of our guilt. God is just and does not exaggerate. Good Friday is what our sins cost.

Forgiven

These words are not meant to demean us. We are beloved by God and raised to life and goodness in Jesus. We are forgiven and made new by faith in His Name. It is the light of this new life that reveals to us the seriousness of sin. We are never to think of our sins as being slight. We need not berate or punish ourselves. We are to be ever mindful that Jesus paid the price in full. Praise His Name!

 Time to Reflect and Journal:

- What stands out for you in these verses?
- What is God's invitation for your life?
- What do you want to answer back to God in prayer?

Silent Saturday
A Time to Wait

 Today's Bible Reading:

Matthew 27:57-66, Mark 15:42-46, Luke 23:50-56, John 19:38-42

Key Memory Verse: Psalm 62:1-2

"For God alone my soul waits in silence; from him comes my salvation. He alone is my rock and my salvation, my fortress; I shall not be greatly shaken."

 Setting the Stage:

Sabbath Eve

The horror of Jesus' crucifixion had come to an end. He died before sunset on Good Friday. The Sabbath began at sunset, so hasty preparations were made for Jesus' burial. Joseph of Arimathea asked for Jesus' body and laid it in a tomb that had been prepared for his own death. Nicodemus assisted in the cost and preparation of the burial. They wrapped the body of Jesus with linen cloth and spices according to custom. But there was more to be done. The Sabbath prevented them from completing the process. Mary and some other women noted the place of His grave and intended to finish the task after the Sabbath. The stone was rolled over the entrance to the tomb, and they all left.

A Time to Wait

The Sabbath (Saturday) was a day to wait. It was time to comfort one another at the loss of Jesus. It was time to face the failures of the moment, in running and denial. The hours were filled with sorting through expectations and disappointments. There were more questions than there were answers. The disciples probably gathered slowly, one by one, perhaps unable at first to look one another in the eye. They were shocked, angry, frightened, confused and deeply pained. But being together was better than being alone. They probably asked, "What now? What do we do?" They didn't know.

Jesus could have been raised from the dead on the Sabbath. Saturday could have been a resurrection day. It wasn't. In place of an immediate resurrection, God chose to wait. We are not told why or what the actions of God were behind the clouds on the Saturday. All we have is an earthly experience of the silence and stillness of death. Earth had to wait for Resurrection Sunday after Good Friday. We had to endure the delay of Saturday. That is God's blessing to us.

We don't like waiting, especially if we wait in pain. Yet the silence of Saturday gives space for us to face our pains, comfort one another, and have our faith enriched. When we don't know what God is doing, when He seems to be silent or inactive, when our confusion is not immediately resolved, when our agendas and expectations are put on hold - this is the time to trust.

We learn an unshakable faith when we are shook. All this is of God. Saturday is the declaration that death has robbed us of our power. Saturday proves that resurrection life is God's to do. We have no say in the timing nor assistance in the doing. All we can do is wait and wait in faith.

A Long Saturday

It's been said that we all are now living in a "prolonged Saturday." We find ourselves between the fact of Jesus' death and the hope of future resurrection. We know that He who was crucified lives, and we wait for our own resurrection. The certainty of what was is our hope for what will be. But it has been over 2000 years. Still, we wait. We wait with pain and death around us. We wait, without every question being answered. We wait, leaning upon the encouragement of one another. We wait for God to do what only God can do. We wait in a prolonged Saturday - but Sunday will come.

 Time to Reflect and Journal:

- What stands out for you in these verses?
- What is God's invitation for your life?
- What do you want to answer back to God in prayer?

Resurrection Sunday
Everything Is Different

 Today's Bible Reading:

Matthew 28:1-20, Mark 16:1-20, Luke 24:1-53, John 20:1 - 21:25

Key Memory Verse: Psalm 47:5-7

"God has gone up with a shout, the Lord with the sound of a trumpet. Sing praises to God, sing praises! Sing praises to our King, sing praises! For God is the King of all the earth; sing praises with a psalm!"

 Setting the Stage:

The Feel of Easter

I have a few theological questions about Easter, mostly surrounding the "How?". Easter can confound with wonder and mystery. So, let's approach an easier question. What did the first Easter morning feel like? The appearances of Jesus solicited a variety of emotions. The women at the tomb are described as filled with "fear and astonishment." The two Emmaus disciples moved from disappointment morphed into astonishment. They were left with burning hearts. The huddled disciples were frightened of authorities and shamed by their running. Jesus appeared and extended peace. For those who loved Jesus, whatever emotions filled their chest, their hearts would be resolved with relief and comfort. Here's why.

I am certain that for the followers of Jesus, His resurrection would feel like a return. Once the fear and bewilderment wore off, they would see Jesus and think, "He has come back!" His re-appearance would be welcomed as a return - a return to normal. They can eat with Him again. They will have walks like they used to. What they lost in His death is now restored with unimaginable relief. All of that is completely understandable.

That's how we all would react if a deceased loved one knocked on our door. All the yesterdays thought gone, have been replaced. The losses have been recovered. It would be relief beyond imagination for Jesus' followers. They've been comforted by a return to what has been. But that is a misunderstanding of Easter. The empty tomb of Jesus is not a replacement of the past. His life is not a return but a resurrection. That became obvious quickly.

Not Yesterday, but Tomorrow

Jesus was different. He was *who* He always was, but not *what* He was. He could appear in a room without using the door. There was something incorporeal about Him, despite having fish for dinner. He was new. He was glorified. When Mary held His legs in the garden, Jesus warned her not to cling to Him. He was not going to stay — and He didn't. The disciples' hope for permanence lasted only 40 days until He left them once more.

If they were looking for the old relationship, they were reminded of Jesus' words about the coming Spirit. They would know Jesus, but now in a new and different way. The point is simple - the resurrection does not restore our yesterdays. It points to our tomorrows.

Even though it occurred 2000 years ago, Easter is future oriented. It's an arrow pointing to what we will be and where we will be. It doesn't take us back to the familiar, but thrusts us towards eternity holding a new heaven and a new earth. We tend to prefer the familiar. Too often we find safety and comfort in what we know. We simply want Jesus to improve it. But He smiles and does more. He makes everything new and then lays all of it at the throne of the Father. So, we get back to the mystery of our theology. I have many questions about what the new will be! But this I know - I want it. I would rather have an unknown future from the resurrected Lord than a re-run of normal.

 Time to Reflect and Journal:

- What stands out for you in these verses?
- What is God's invitation for your life?
- What do you want to answer back to God in prayer?

Passion Week Ended

You have trod over familiar territory this week. You've read Scriptures that you have read before. But walking with Jesus is never rote. Perhaps He granted you fresh insight into His grace. You may have expressed a deeper gratitude and understanding of His mercy. We trust that you recognized His presence and Voice through your prayers. You may choose to review this week and glean the sustenance He sent you. May God continue to lead you along your spiritual journey. The week is over, but our walk continues!

It may be for some, that this is your first time reading the story of Jesus' suffering, death, and resurrection. It's more than a story. It is an invitation. All of this happened for you. Jesus died that you might be forgiven. He was raised that you might live with Him forever! We answer His invitation by turning to the Saviour and away from "best efforts." We can trust His mercy to forgive and grace to make us new. Like the thief crucified beside Jesus, we admit our guilt and believe Jesus can rescue us. Today, you can find the assurance, *"You will be with Me in paradise!"*

REFLECTIONS

REFLECTIONS